PUFFIN BOOKS

50 Questions Your Dog Would Ask Its Vet
(*If Your Dog Could Talk*)

Bruce Fogle, DVM, MRCVS, is a practising vet, and lectures on animal behaviour at veterinary colleges internationally. He has written several books on the behavioural problems of pets.

BRUCE FOGLE
DVM, MRCVS

50 Questions Your Dog Would Ask Its Vet

(If Your Dog Could Talk)

Illustrated by Paul Davies

PUFFIN BOOKS

PUFFIN BOOKS

Published by the Penguin Group
Penguin Books Ltd, 27 Wrights Lane, London W8 5TZ, England
Penguin Books USA Inc., 375 Hudson Street, New York, New York 10014, USA
Penguin Books Australia Ltd, Ringwood, Victoria, Australia
Penguin Books Canada Ltd, 10 Alcorn Avenue, Toronto, Ontario, Canada M4V 3B2
Penguin Books (NZ) Ltd, 182–190 Wairau Road, Auckland 10, New Zealand

Penguin Books Ltd, Registered Offices: Harmondsworth, Middlesex, England

First published as *101 Questions Your Dog Would Ask Its Vet (If Your Dog Could Talk)* by
Michael Joseph Ltd 1993
Published in this edition Puffin Books 1994
1 3 5 7 9 10 8 6 4 2

Typeset by Datix International Limited, Bungay, Suffolk
Set in 13/14 pt Monophoto Goudy
Printed in England by Clays Ltd, St Ives plc

Contents

Acknowledgements

The more time I spend with them – and, professionally speaking, it is now well over twenty years – the more I like dogs. I respect them, but also they make me laugh. And so, first of all, my apologies to any dogs or their people who might think, after reading some of these questions, that I'm not taking them seriously. I hope you'll see from the answers that I am. And second, my thanks and acknowledgement to the thousands of dog owners who, over the years, have asked the questions that follow. Thanks, too, to the dogs.

Introduction

It might seem silly having dogs ask questions. In fact it IS silly. After all, they can't speak and we can only guess at what they are thinking. But I've had dogs ask questions in this book for an important reason – to remind you that they have feelings and emotions too, just like we do.

If you have a dog you probably treat him or her as part of the family. And although your pet can't talk, you can tell when your canine friend is happy or sad or just plain grumpy. That's because dogs and people 'talk' with their bodies in similar ways. Dogs that think they are tough strut their stuff, just like some people do. Dogs that feel happy bounce around and want to play, just like we do. As a veterinarian, my patients can't tell me in words how they feel, but I can tell by watching their 'body language'.

All of us who have pets have a responsibility for them. We have to protect them from danger and care for them when they aren't well. To do so we have to understand what they are telling us silently with their expressions, their body movements and their behaviour. It's exciting to understand this language because when you do you really know how and why your dog behaves the way he or she does.

What you discover is that dogs are not furry people in disguise. They might act almost human because they live with us and are trained by us from the time they are born. But without that training they behave as they really are – wolves in disguise. Even with good training your dog's behaviour still is that of the wolf. When you read these questions and answers you will see how similar dogs and wolves actually are.

CHAPTER ONE
Instincts and Communication

1. I want to be the pack leader with people. How should I go about it?

Disobey. Even the puniest, most insignificant dog can become the pack leader with humans because people are such pushovers.

People often don't notice the first signs of a dog's attempt to become leader of the pack. They think it is cute when, as a pup, he growls at people. They pay little attention when he first disregards a command to 'come' and continues to do whatever he is doing. They willingly offer him something else to eat when he refuses to eat what he has been given.

Pack leadership can be achieved without showing open aggression. Small dogs, for example, can pester until they are picked up, can choose to jump up on furniture or even crawl under the covers on people's beds. By doing these things, they become the decision makers. Because they look delicate, it might appear that these dogs are leading from behind, but the ploy is so successful that some people dramatically alter their lifestyles, hiring dog sitters if they go out for the evening and totally avoiding yearly holidays so that their dog need not go into kennels.

As pack animals, all dogs feel most comfortable knowing where they stand in the pecking order of the pack. Although sex, size and breed are significant factors, any dog has the potential to become pack leader. People are often psychologically prepared to defend their leadership positions from obvious candidates like muscular male Akitas, but drop their guard when confronted by less obvious challengers.

2. Why do I compulsively feel the need to roll on dead fish, fox droppings and anything else that people find repulsive?

Just as many people enjoy masking their personal body odours with artificial ones, so do dogs. Dogs find certain odours appealing, and usually

prefer the smell of decomposing organic material, such as leaf mould, rotting fish and fertilizer.

Applying canine perfume is almost always performed in a ritual manner. If a dog simply wants to have a playful roll he will quite carelessly throw himself on his back – sometimes even somersaulting to do so – and, arching left and right, kick his legs up in the air. He then gets up and trots along.

When applying perfume, however, a dog is much more particular. He carefully sniffs his chosen cologne. If it is 'bottled', like dead fish, he might carry it from the beach on to the grass and lay it out in an exact manner. Then quite studiously, like a human applying perfume behind one ear and then the other, he rubs on his substance with one shoulder and then the other. At this stage he might not even roll. Instead he inhales the perfume once more and, reinvigorated by the aroma, applies the substance once more to his shoulders and then, using a full roll, to his back. This is a clever move for an animal that in the wild must stalk and kill other animals in order to survive. If he masks his own odour and is up-wind to a potential meal, that meal will probably not be too concerned if it thinks it is being approached by a dead fish.

3. Sometimes I get so excited when people come home that I wet myself. How can I learn to control my bladder?

Dogs who wet themselves when they greet people lack self-esteem. To stop doing it they need to gain confidence.

People should always be at the top of the totem pole in the dog pack hierarchy. All dogs should demonstrate submissiveness when their people come home, but a simple wag of the tail is all that is really needed. More open displays of faithfulness to human leaders – whining, grovelling, rolling over or, worst, rolling over and urinating – are unnecessary.

15

Often unwittingly people reassert their leadership by reaching down from their considerable height and patting the dog on the top of the head. If people act this way with an insecure dog, she wets herself. To correct the problem people should avoid touching the insecure dog immediately; instead, they should come in the house without making eye contact. After a few minutes they should stoop to reduce their height and, still avoiding eye contact, put forward an upturned palm and let the dog make the decision to come forward. When she does come forward, the person tickles her under the chin but still doesn't look at her or speak to her. Perfectly natural human greeting rituals, such as eye contact and verbal 'hallos', are gestures of dominance to dogs. If people avoid using them, the insecure dog has a chance to improve her self-worth. When she does that, she learns to control her bladder too.

4. Why do I feel the need to bark so loudly when strangers approach the house? Humans have threatened me with debarking.

Any sensible dog considers himself to be a member of a pack and his house to be the most important part of his pack's territory. Although the role of the pack leaders always goes to humans, all members of the pack are equally responsible for warning others when their territory is about to be invaded. And the best way to warn all others instantly is to bark.

For thousands of years humans have interfered in dog breeding, turning the comparatively quiet wolf into the yapping dog. Because a dog's hearing is about four times more acute than a human's, dogs make good guards. Now, after intentionally selecting for and enhancing barking, humans have decided that it is a dog trait they don't particularly want.

Some breeds bark more than others. Generally speaking, small dogs, especially terriers, are yappers, while large dogs, especially gun dogs, are relatively quiet. Debarking is an operation in which holes are punched in the dog's vocal cords. Except in Japan, where barking is the worst crime a dog can commit, very few veterinarians are ever willing to carry out the operation. Instead vets suggest finding out why the dog feels the need to bark and then retraining him accordingly. When this proves impossible, they might try a curious bark-stopping method developed in France that involves the dog wearing a special collar containing a vial of citronella. When the dog barks, a microchip in the collar is activated and the lemon scent of citronella envelops the barker. This innocuous smell acts as an instant distraction. In a short period of time many dogs will not bark whenever they are wearing their personal odour-maker.

5. Why do I howl when I hear Beethoven?

Howling is a form of communication. Dogs howl to tell each other where they are. Whether they are trying to communicate with Beethoven when they howl is questionable, however.

Wolves use the howl to speak to each other. When, for example, a pack is dispersed in the woods and a lonely wolf pup yips a 'Where is everbody?' yip, eerie, primitive, plaintive and quite beautiful howls respond. The pup stops yipping. Young dogs also yip when left alone. As they mature some dogs, especially hounds and Dobermanns, develop mournful howls. When they are lonely they turn their heads skywards, purse their lips and bay.

Loneliness is not the only reason for howling. Some dogs howl when greeting people. Others howl when they are happy, and some howl to music. A dog's hearing range is about the same as a human's, roughly eight and a half octaves, but their sensitivity within that range is quite acute.

They can, for example, differentiate between two notes differing by only one-eighth of a tone. This explains why dogs learn to respond to a shepherd's whistled commands so easily.

Deep in one of the most basic parts of their brains humans have a music centre. Dogs probably do too. Music is relaxing. It can be calming and reassuring to animals. Howling to Beethoven – or to any other music for that matter – is always actively performed by the howler: a dog joins in because he wants to. It's enjoyable. If the sound of music were unpleasant, he would simply get up and leave.

6. I live with a cat and enjoy her company, so why do I always feel this urge to chase any other cat I see?

Dogs instinctively chase anything that moves fast, especially if it is small and furry, but when personal relationships develop they usually draw the line. When a dog and cat live together, the cat usually dominates. If a dog becomes too nosy or inquisitive, a confident cat hisses, spits and swipes her canine companion into line. In good, stable relationships, the cat will sleep contentedly with the dog, eat in the same room at the same time, and use a wagging tail as a plaything and the dog's forelimbs as scratching posts. Dogs are usually fascinated by cats and allow them to do all these things.

Strange cats are treated differently. When there are no formal relationships, dogs chase cats just as dogs chase squirrels. This is an instinctive reaction at the very base of dog behaviour and is independent of sex, age or hunger. Rapid movement stimulates the chase. This can put a pet at risk, especially if she lives with two or more canines. Even when dogs are on perfectly amicable terms with a cat, the dogs can go native and chase their friend if they see her run. This is less likely to happen in a single-dog household.

Chasing is a good game, but the great risk comes from the fact that it is self-perpetuating. Chasing stimulates a rush of adrenalin. Dogs find that invigorating, so when they are offered the opportunity, they will chase again. The more often they chase, the more likely they are to catch a cat, and possibly even to kill it.

7. I enjoyed watching television when I lived in Europe, but now that I have moved to America all I see is a blur. What has happened to my eyes?

Television is better for dogs to watch in Europe than in North America. Aside from the fact that in Europe dogs are more likely than those in North America to see sheepdog trials, show jumping and natural history shows – all favourite programmes – differences in transmission quality mean that dogs see TV pictures in Europe but only dots in America.

Until high-definition television becomes readily available, American dogs are restricted to watching an inferior system that transmits pictures so slowly all they see are dots on the screen. If these unfortunate canines hear Lassie, Benji or Rin Tin Tin barking, they look behind the television to see where the dog is.

European dogs have no difficulty seeing television images because both kinds of European TV transmission system are faster than the American one, fast enough to form images that dogs can see. This means that if there is a good programme on TV, the European dog will settle down and watch it. People need not invest in colour TV, however. Although dogs have cells in their eyes and in their brains that can form colour images, they are completely uninterested in colour and are happy to see in shades of grey.

8. Why do I dig so many holes in the ground and then just leave them?

Digging is both mentally and physically stimulating. This form of open-face mining is a dead-end behaviour in many dogs. They do it because it is

an instinctive behaviour that once served a useful purpose.

Although wolves classically feast on large herbivores, such as deer, they also eat a surprisingly large number of small rodents. Wolves use a cat-like pounce to capture wandering rodents. However, rather than sit patiently at a den as a cat will when she is waiting for her meal to emerge, the typical wolf uses his forepaws to dig where the rodent has gone to ground until he finds his prey. This is one reason why dogs dig holes and leave them.

Because in the wild there are times when food is plentiful and other times when food is scarce, wolves often hide excess food. When stomachs have been filled, they dig in the earth and bury parts of carcasses for future consumption. Dogs do this with bones, of course, but today few are given bones to chew. The desire to bury food remains, so on a full stomach a dog might dig a hole but, having nothing to drop in it, will simply leave it.

Dogs also dig out of boredom, or to escape, but in the end they do it because it stimulates the senses. As well as refreshing the muscles, digging releases a cornucopia of smells from the ground, many of which are organic in origin and lip-smackingly good. Worms, bugs, decomposing matter, moisture: all of these are a delight to the inquisitive canine's senses.

9. I've been told that sometimes when I am asleep my face twitches and my legs flail in the air. Apparently I cry or howl. What's happening?

Dogs dream more vividly than most humans. They rest frequently during the day, often falling into a light but alert sleep from which they instantly emerge when any of their senses are stimulated. Bored dogs will sleep more deeply during the day and, just as they do at night, will experience periods of deep sleep during which they dream.

As pack members, dogs co-ordinate their activities with their humans. Because humans enjoy prolonged night-time sleeping, most dogs do the same, although if given preference they would prefer to be up at the crack of dawn. As dogs go from light sleep to deep sleep their eyes start to move under their closed lids. This happens to people too. Electrical changes occur in the brains of both dogs and humans; while most people dream quietly, dogs dream more robustly. First their whiskers twitch, then their lips move and sometimes their jaws chew and their tongues lick. At the same time, their paw muscles retract and they start paddling with their feet, making Disneyesque running movements. Some utter short crying yips or howls. Although human dreams last about twenty minutes, dog dreams are much shorter – either the rabbit is caught or it is not. The dog then falls back into a light sleep but will dream several more times before the night is out.

10. Why do I sometimes feel the urge to bite people's ankles just when they're about to leave the room?

This is a curious learned behaviour and is a simple but effective expression of canine bossiness. When people gather together in the

presence of an ankle-biting dog, they might think the dog is an irrelevant member of the household, but the dog thinks he is the supremo. He likes to think that he is the centre of activity and that people have gathered for his benefit.

He might behave perfectly normally, offering sociable greetings to everyone, chatting about the weather, asking about the kids and being generously affectionate, allowing people – even asking them – to stroke him and talk to him. A perfect host. But as they leave he undergoes a complete personality change. He has enjoyed the company and doesn't want it to end, but people are leaving without his permission. So he eats ankle.

The procedure is rewarding because it is so effective: bite a departing ankle and you not only become the centre of attention and assert your authority, but you also delay your guests from leaving. That is why dogs will do the same thing on the next visit from humans. People can prevent this form of canine dominance either by not letting the dog mix with company or, quite simply, by removing him well before their human guests depart.

CHAPTER TWO
Emotions and Behaviour

11. I know I'm loved, but I still feel jealous when I see people petting the old dog I live with. So I bit him. How can I control this selfish side of myself?

Rivalry amongst dogs is natural but should never lead to problems as long as people acknowledge the top dog first and then lower members of the pack. Unfortunately, one of the problems humans have is that they naturally feel more responsibility for the underdog and unwittingly create problems for her.

In a typical household, people might already have a dog when they acquire a new puppy. At first, the original dog remains dominant through size and seniority. But then, as the pup matures and the first dog ages, a time might come when the newcomer feels it is his turn to become top dog. People quite naturally continue to pat the

original first, but this annoys the second dog and leads to fights. When dogs fight in front of humans, but never in their absence, it is almost certain they are disputing for attention from their people.

To overcome this type of jealousy, people should observe the natural changes occurring in pack seniority and then reinforce these changes by always acknowledging the dominant dog first. Their hearts might find this a difficult practice, but it will instantly eliminate further acts of jealousy.

12. Each time I see the new people next door I growl and threaten. There is just something about them that I don't like. My humans don't like my behaviour. How can I control it?

Some dogs are deeply suspicious of anything or anybody new. Neighbours, in particular, can be troublesome because they remain so close to a dog's territory and never go away. They are constantly threatening. If they have a dog, the threat is even more real.

This type of problem is, in fact, quite easy to overcome. All that is necessary is for the threatened dog to think that the new neighbours and their dogs are simply new members of an extended pack. The dogs and neighbours should meet first on neutral territory, in the local park for example. The dog will see that these new people and their dog are no threat to his humans. The dog can be offered a little food by the neighbours, and if there are even the remotest signs of canine aggression the dog should be firmly told off.

Once the neighbours and their dog are able to meet in the park with no troubles, they proceed to meet on the dog's home territory, both outside and inside. It takes a very short time for a dog to accept that there is no threat intended from the new humans and only a little longer to accept that the new canine isn't a threat either.

13. I'm mean and nasty. What type of muzzle should I use?

Muzzles should allow a dog to pant freely or even to drink but should prevent her from biting. Any dog should be muzzled if she is placed in a situation where she might bite. The softest, gentlest canine might bite when she is in pain. If a dog has been injured, she should be muzzled temporarily while she is taken to the veterinary clinic.

Members of breeds that are known to be potentially snappy should always be muzzled when they first meet crawling children. Kids don't mean to hurt dogs, but it is no fun to be yanked by your hair, and a typical terrier's response is to snap at the yanker. Only when people are convinced that there are no dangers should an unmuzzled dog be allowed to be with young children and then only in the presence of adults.

Some dogs are unpredictable, and they should be muzzled whenever they are off their own territory. This means they should wear a muzzle when visiting the veterinary clinic, when exercising, when being walked and whenever they are off the lead. Some people like to put heavy studded leather muzzles on their dogs. These are unpleasant for dogs and unnecessary. Instead, dogs should wear either a basket-like muzzle that allows complete air circulation, or a nylon cone-like one that slips on the nose but allows enough space for the tongue to come out for panting or lapping. Dogs initially don't like wearing muzzles, but if they are introduced to them gently, they soon accept them.

31

14. Recently there was an upset in my life and my favourite person is no longer here. Now all I want to do is lie around looking miserable. Is this dog depression?

Yes, it is. Dogs have emotions and suffer from depression just as humans do. What dogs enjoy most is constancy. They form emotional attachments to other dogs and to people, and can be very upset when these attachments are broken.

That doesn't mean that all dogs get depressed when there are major changes in their lives. Once more, just like people, some adapt better than others. Those most likely to suffer are dogs that have formed deep dependent relationships with one person or one dog in particular. In other words, followers are more likely to become depressed than leaders. The problem can be reduced by ensuring that dogs treat all human members of their pack as co-leaders, so that when one is absent there is another to whom the dog can show allegiance.

Temporary separations cause only temporary depression but permanent separation is more difficult for a dog to understand. Although the value is questionable, there is no harm in letting a surviving dog see and sniff the body of another household pet that has died recently. When people die or move away, another person should immediately take over leadership responsibilities, making sure that the dog receives affection, touch, nourishment and discipline. When this is done, depression lasts only a short time and virtually never requires medical treatment.

15. I hate being left alone, so when it happens I rampage through the house to amuse myself. But why do I also eat houseplants, chew furniture and urinate on the bed?

Dogs are very sociable animals. They relish activity, not necessarily because they want to participate in it, although most do, but because just watching is mentally stimulating. Unless a dog is unwell, or really prefers to be in the background, he wants to be in the middle of the action. When people have other people over to the house the dog wants to greet and investigate them, join them for drinks and help with the barbecue. He doesn't like being left out.

Being left alone is unnatural and boring. Dogs living with humans soon learn that when they are bored they need only search out another member of the human pack and they will be touched, talked to, played with, fed, or even admonished – this, too, is a form of attention. Attention is what dogs want. When the entire human pack leaves the dog alone he becomes anxious, agitated and frustrated. In his anxiety he becomes destructive.

His destructive activities are not carried out in revenge for being left alone. For instance, he doesn't say to himself that he's going to urinate on the bed because he knows humans find this deeply offensive. He does things he would never do otherwise, out of anxiety and frustration. To avoid these problems, people should accustom dogs, while they are still very young pups, to be left alone. People should depart quietly, without saying 'goodbye' or making physical contact – dogs are clever at hearing hidden stress in people's voices. Two or three chewable toys should be left for the dog to play with. Leaving a radio or television on might also provide soothing background noise and help to reduce his natural anxiety to an acceptable level.

16. I am a happy and content fourteen-year-old. My people have recently decided they are going to get a puppy for me. Is this really necessary?

In most instances a new pup does wonders for an elderly dog and the family too. All dogs, even those that are firmly convinced they are human and that other dogs are aliens from outer space, ultimately enjoy canine companionship. With the exception of dogs who show senile changes or are in chronic discomfort with old age aches and pains, even dogs who have never experienced the company of another of their own kind will, within days or weeks, thank their humans for bringing into the pack something they completely understand.

An elderly dog initially does not like being leapt upon, licked, sucked, nuzzled, pummelled and chewed by a pup. He will snap at the youngster, who soon learns that the elderly deserve respect. On the other hand, pups smell delicious, they speak in much better dog language than people ever can and they act as a fountain of youth, bringing out a streak of competitiveness and playfulness in the old one.

The life expectancy of the canine old age pensioner is limited, but his death is slightly easier for people when there is another dog in the home stirring up the silent air. There is, however, a critical point in canine ageing after which it is unwise for people to bring home a new pup. If an elderly dog is irreversibly mentally or physically infirm, it is best to wait until after his departure before puppifying the house.

17. Lately I've been irritable. Am I getting grumpier as I get older?

Irritability often increases with advancing age, but it frequently has a specific and treatable cause.

As life progresses, dogs become quite settled in their ways. Routine becomes more and more important, until eventually dogs will carry out specific activities, not necessarily because they want to do them but just because they have always done them. A dog might bark an 'I'm irritated' demand that he wants to go outside because he has always gone outside at that time, but once out he forgets why he wanted to go there.

With ageing, a dog's senses diminish. Like humans he doesn't hear as well as he used to, and just like people he certainly can't focus his eyes as he once could. All the nerves in his body become less efficient; they don't send messages as quickly as they did. This means that sudden sights and sounds are more likely to frighten him. An unexpected touch becomes fear-inducing, and he responds with a snap of his teeth. These perfectly natural ageing changes can lead to a certain grumpiness.

Irritability might also be caused by chronic low-grade discomfort. Dogs are not complainers. They simply get on with life even when they develop bone, joint and muscle weakness or pain. If it hurts when they move, they have every right to snap when people stroke them. Fortunately, this type of grumpiness frequently responds to anti-inflammatories or other appropriate medicines.

18. I'm well fed and well cared for, but I still hate anyone coming near my food or my toys. Is this what humans call obsessive behaviour? Can it lead to problems?

It is not an obsession. It is simply guarding behaviour, a form of jealousy. Some dogs guard their food, others their toys, and still others their people. All of these activities can lead to serious problems.

Guarding is more common in some breeds than others. It occurs with surprising frequency in golden retrievers, a breed renowned for gentleness of spirit. Male goldens in particular can be very possessive of food bowls, never allowing humans or canines near them. Many terriers act in a similar fashion, but primarily with their

toys. This is a form of possessive aggression. Other variations include competition for affection from people or sibling rivalry.

Because possessiveness is a form of dog dominance and because there is a strong genetic component in the condition, prevention means selecting the right breed when you choose your pet. For example, possessiveness isn't a serious problem with pack hounds like beagles, who are bred to work together. Treating the problem means that people have to assert their authority by revealing their own dominance, especially when the dog is still young. All human members of the family must take part in commanding the dog to obey instructions such as 'sit' and 'stay'. By reducing the dog's self-confidence, people reassert their authority over him and he will become less authoritarian about his possessions.

19. I enjoy meeting people. In fact, I think they are a marvellous species. But why is it that I can't seem to get on with my own kind?

People often get dogs when the pups are around eight weeks old and then keep them in dog-free environments for the following month, during which the canines are inoculated against infectious diseases. Unfortunately this is one of the most important months in the dog's entire life, for it is during this time that he acquires important knowledge about the world around him.

Between eight and twelve weeks of age a dog learns the basic social graces. Most importantly, he learns the right and wrong way to meet other dogs. If, for example, he stays with his mother and irritates her, she bites him in a forceful yet careful way and he learns that there are limits to boisterousness. But in the absence of dog-to-dog encounters during this critical socializing period, he is likely to forget what he learned with his litter and instead learns how to behave socially only with humans. All sensible dogs must learn about human culture, but at the same time they need to know as much as possible about how to behave with other dogs if they are ever to enjoy dog company. This means that even before they are fully vaccinated, pups should continue to meet other healthy dogs. If this is done, the pup will mature into an adult equally at ease with humans and other canines.

CHAPTER THREE
Training

20. *What forms of discipline might people use to train me and how can I best resist?*

Rewards and discipline are used equally in dog training. Food and physical contact are the best rewards, while social isolation and harsh words are punishments. Sometimes, although very rarely, physical punishment is used. In all but the most exceptional circumstances it is in the dog's best interests to allow herself to be trained simply because trained dogs almost invariably enjoy safer and more secure lives.

Food is a powerful reward – so powerful that

some dogs will forget they are being trained in order to get it. In these circumstances people should instead use touch as their reward. Different touches mean different things. A simple pat or stroke is all that is needed when a dog is rewarded for good work. Words of praise work well too, but not as well as food or touch. Using positive rewards is a far better way to train a dog than using punishing discipline.

When dogs develop behaviour problems, however, discipline is needed. The very worst behaviour, like sheep-chasing, can only be altered by discipline so powerful that it is greater than the thrill the dog gets from the chase. This is one of the rare situations where, with professional help, people might use a shock collar on a dog. For less serious crimes, verbal threats, unexpected frights from noises, and physical isolation for two minutes at most are very effective and frequently successful methods to reinforce training.

21. I love chasing sheep but I'm told the farmer has a gun and the right to use it on me. How can I stop behaving like some wild animal?

It is difficult to stop doing what nature intended you to do. The thrills are so enormous, and the rewards so magnificent, that only the most dramatic intervention will stop sheep-chasing.

Dogs instinctively chase anything that moves, and sheep are so defenceless and so dumb that they make perfect victims. Their rapid movements when fearful bring out the primitive in many canines. Dogs who have never before harmed even a grasshopper suddenly feel a deep-seated urge to chase and bite. In a matter of minutes the gentlest of human companions can leave war-like carnage throughout a field, tearing and disembowelling his way through a flock.

Shepherds know that early learning is the best

method of prevention, which is why they sometimes put sheepdog pups in a pen with a protective ewe and her lambs. Nothing is as awesome as a mother protecting her young, and a pup quickly learns never to bite, even playfully, and to leave *all* sheep alone. When dogs are near sheep they should always be kept on leads. If a dog has chased sheep in the past, only the most dramatic form of retraining will work. The thrill of the chase must be countermanded by such strong discipline that a dog will think twice about chasing again. This is one of the very few instances where people should consider getting professional assistance to use a remote control shock collar to help eliminate this lethal pursuit.

22. Can toys really be intellectually stimulating?

Good toys provide mental and physical stimulation, but the best mimic reality.

Balls, Frisbees and eccentrically bouncing 'kongs' are all 'chase' toys. Just as a dog will chase a potential meal, she chases these objects as they try to escape. The most realistic escapers are kongs. Because of their odd shape, they bounce this way and that unexpectedly, just as a rabbit would run. This provides real-life exercise for the dog for, rather than running in a straight line, she must be constantly alert to changes of direction.

Toys with squeakers are for killing. The dog often pounces upon these and gives them a quick chew – just as she would do to a mouse.

Hard toys, like nylon rings and rawhide wraps, are for chewing. These exercise the teeth and gums. The front incisor teeth scrape, the large canine teeth hold, and the side molar teeth crush. Few dogs ever get a chance to do these perfectly natural things with food because their meals come out of packages. An additional advantage of this type of toy is that it teaches physical skill. Dogs learn to be so nimble with their forepaws that some people swear they have thumbs.

Finally, there are tug-of-war toys. People enjoy playing with these, not realizing that dogs play with them not for intellectual stimulation but simply to win and to show authority over people. All toys remain the property of people. Tug-of-war toys in particular must always be given back to the owners at the end of a game.

23. What early training should my pups have to ensure they grow up to be all-rounders?

From as early an age as possible pups should have all their senses routinely stimulated. They should meet a variety of different animals and people of all sizes. They should travel in cars and walk through pedestrian traffic. Occasionally they should be left alone for a few hours, but they should also be invited to people's parties. The more they experience between birth and twelve weeks of age, the larger their brains will grow and the greater will be the number of inter-connections between cells in their brains.

Pups don't have the option of picking who their mothers will be, but mothers do imprint a whole range of behaviours on their pups. Unsure mothers are more likely to produce whining pups, while stern disciplinarians are more likely to produce more introverted pups. What makes early puppyhood so completely different from early childhood is that pups are taken away from their mothers and raised by another species. The disadvantage is that it interferes with natural learning; the advantage is that people can teach pups more than their mothers ever could.

Early stimulation of the senses means that a dog is less likely to be frightened by the new or unusual when he is older. That is why dogs raised in cities are almost always less fearful of strangers or strange situations than dogs raised in rural areas. All-rounders should start learning about life – under human supervision – as soon as they want to start exploring.

24. How much daily exercise should I have? Should I run free or remain on a lead?

The amount of exercise a dog requires varies with his age, breed and early experience. It does not depend on his size: some large or giant dogs need much less exercise than medium, small or even miniature dogs. Once a dog has been fully trained to 'stay' or 'come' on command, he should enjoy having his daily exercise off his lead.

Dogs are keen observers of nature. Given the opportunity, a typical dog prefers spending his time outdoors listening to bird-song, watching bugs and smelling any scents that waft his way. Just like humans, many dogs act as if they are slightly distanced from the raw naturalness of the world around them, as though they themselves are of a higher and more dignified order. Other dogs, when offered the choice of lush green grass or a warm sofa on which to while away their lives, choose the sofa.

Homebodies don't need less exercise than green dogs: both need to exercise their bodies fully each day, preferably by running. Ideally dogs should visit different places for their exercise because new places are more stimulating. New sights, sounds and smells are invigorating. However, people should be more careful when letting dogs off their leads in these new settings.

25. What are the best types of collar, harness and lead for me?

A dog's wardrobe varies with her age, breed and general behaviour. Rolled leather collars are excellent because they are unlikely to damage fur on the neck, although soft, flat nylon collars are almost equally gentle to the fur. Poorly made flat leather collars with rough edges are more likely to wear down neck fur; heavy metal collars can do the same. A couple of human fingers should fit under a properly tightened collar. On this garment a dog should wear her necessary identification, including name, telephone number and, where legislation requires it, her vaccination status.

A harness can be better than a collar, especially for thick-necked breeds like pugs or for Yorkshire terriers, who sometimes have delicate windpipes. The lead is attached to the top of the harness so that there is no pressure on the neck if the dog pulls either forward or back. A horse halter-like apparatus is ideal for boisterous or unreliable dogs. The lead is attached under the chin on the dog halter, which means that if the dog unexpectedly lunges forward, the momentum pulls her nose down towards the ground and shuts her jaws.

Extendable leads are better than fixed-length ones but only if people use them properly. When walking to or from the exercise area, these leads

should be locked in a short-lead position, but once the dog and her human reach the right area, the extension can be let out, allowing the dog to explore safely. With good training, the sensible canine can then be released.

26. How can I train people to play fetch with me?

People really like playing fetch with dogs so it isn't difficult to train them. A natural inclination by both parties is necessary, however. Lazy and sedentary people and dogs are not interested in this game. Nor are scent-obsessed dogs, which is why it is more difficult to train a nosy blood-hound than a fawning Labrador.

Retrievable objects should be easy to throw and should fit neatly and safely in a dog's mouth. Tennis balls are ideal for all but the smallest dogs because they are firm yet soft and unlikely to cause damage. Golf balls, although an ideal size for small dogs, are too hard and if caught in flight can break a dog's teeth. Kongs are excellent because they bounce so erratically. Frisbees should only be used with lightweight dogs; heavyset or overweight dogs can tear leg ligaments by jumping high in the air to capture sailing Frisbees.

The sensible dog drops an object at a person's feet and kindly but firmly requests that person to throw it. If the dog is a dedicated chewer, she should be on an extended lead and the object should be thrown only a short distance. That way, if the dog does not bring back the object but settles down for a chew instead, she can be reeled in and rewarded with a snack or a stroke for releasing it. It takes most dogs only a very short time to realize that it is more fun to retrieve and return than to retrieve and chew. Verbal rewards then take over, and the training of both parties is complete.

CHAPTER FOUR
Diet

27. *Will neutering make me fat and boring?*

If calories are not watched, neutering can definitely make a dog fat, but not boring.

In both males and females the sex cycle uses up calories. Dogs obviously burn up energy when looking for sex, but they also use calories to make eggs and sperm. Both the oestrous cycle in females and sex-related aggression and territory patrol in males are energy-consuming. When a dog is neutered these energy demands drop. The amount of food eaten should drop too.

Neutering does alter certain male behaviours, but the changes are interesting rather than boring. Most neutered males don't feel as great a need to urine-mark their territories. Less urine-marking makes them more appealing human companions, so they find they are disciplined less and played with more. Similarly, neutering reduces vagrancy and sex-related male-to-male aggression. Less of these behaviours means less danger. Neutering does not diminish any form of aggression or reduce a dog's natural inquisitiveness, it simply pushes sex down from the top priority a dog has and allows other activities like hunting, tracking, retrieving, or playing games to become more prominent.

If a dog is to be neutered, people should make sure that they watch that dog's calories for several months after the operation. A simple rule is to reduce calorie intake by ten per cent immediately after neutering. A drop of twenty-five per cent is quite normal but only becomes necessary if weight is gained.

28. I crave rabbit droppings. Horse manure makes my mouth water. I can't resist dipping into the cat's litter tray. I even eat my own droppings. Am I sick?

All of these are perfectly normal canine habits. Dogs have a natural, even healthy, interest in droppings, but people often find this interest quite disgusting.

Unlike cats, who prefer their food as fresh as possible, dogs willingly eat rotten flesh. Taste is important to dogs but not as important as it is to people. Dogs have far fewer taste-buds; rather than delicately registering sweet and sour, bitter or salty, they probably register general reactions like pleasant, indifferent and unpleasant. The smell and texture of food is more important than taste – droppings smell and feel divine.

Manure, especially herbivore manure, is nutritious for dogs. It often contains nutrients and enzymes that are useful in canine digestion. Puppies, especially fast-growing puppies, usually first eat droppings as an experiment. They get pleasure from finding them and tasting them. If the exercise is rewarding, and that can mean either the

droppings taste good or the pup gets lots of attention from people this way, the initial experiment becomes a habit. Sometimes dogs will eat droppings because they have a lack of digestive enzymes. If this is the case, people should increase the dog's diet with either enzyme supplements or enzyme-containing foods such as pineapple, pumpkin, vegetable marrow or papaya fruit.

29. Sometimes I pass such foul wind that even I have to leave the room. How can I control it?

Intestinal gas is produced by gas-forming bacteria, and the number of bacteria will vary with the food that is eaten. Altering the diet is the most sensible way for a dog to become more socially acceptable.

Flatulence is often associated with eating vegetables like beans and peas, but a wide variety of different foods will stimulate these bacteria to

multiply in a dog's gastrointestinal system. In
fact, there are no hard and fast rules about which
diets make dogs windy. In theory, diets high in
roughage should do so, while high-protein diets
should not. In practice, however, high-protein,
all-meat diets can turn some dogs into gas fac-
tories, while poor-quality, high-roughage diets
don't.

Antibiotics sometimes cause dogs to pass foul
wind because they upset the bacterial balance in
the gut. When this happens, feeding yoghurt that
contains 'nice' live bacteria can rectify the problem. In other circumstances dogs should alter
their eating habits, trying various combinations
of foods, each for a couple of weeks at a time, to
find out which ones result in the best-formed
stools with the least gas. If a dog wants to stick to
the diet he likes, live yoghurt or special 'nice'
bacteria-containing nutritional aids can be mixed
in his food supplements to aid digestion and
improve social acceptability.

30. People feed me the same things at the same time day after day. Shouldn't I have a more varied diet?

If a diet is perfectly well balanced there is no
harm in a dog eating the same food for her entire
life. This puts a lot of faith in the food preparer's

ability to make sure every vitamin, trace mineral, essential fatty acid and amino acid is present in just the right quantity, so varying the diet does no harm and might even do good.

Dogs often get very settled in their ways. They enjoy routine and this can include knowing that they get fed with a certain food at certain times each day. Frequency is quite important. Anatomically dogs are built to gorge once or twice a week and then live off the large reserve sitting in the stomach. Given their preference, they enjoy eating more frequently, at least once or twice a day. This frequency is set up early in life. Later on it will be easy to increase, but upsetting for the dogs if it is reduced. From a nutritional viewpoint the number of meals each day is irrelevant: the number of daily calories is the most important factor.

Occasionally changing brands or even the texture of food from dry, soft-moist or canned can be exciting for some dogs but cause diarrhoea in others. An alternative is to stick to what a dog likes but to add a vitamin and mineral supplement to her diet. Nutritionally these are probably quite unnecessary but they taste good, can be used as rewards during training, may fill an unknown gap in her nutritional intake and, when given in recommended amounts, can do no harm.

31. Even though I am well fed, and if anything even a little bit overweight, why do I have this constant need to scavenge?

Searching for food, or scavenging as it is also known, is fun. It is real dog work. It is exciting and rewarding. A dog can use his senses to do what they were meant to do: search, investigate and consume. Like wealthy business people who do deals not because they need more money but because of the thrill of doing deals, dogs scavenge not because they need more food but because of the thrill that comes from scavenging. That is why even well-fed dogs willingly scavenge.

Boredom is an integral part of scavenging. Working dogs, such as search and rescue, police and guide dogs, who must concentrate their minds on other activities, are less likely to scavenge than sedentary couch lizards. For the majority of pet dogs, however, a daily outing to a park or recreation area is the highlight of the day; it is the only time that all the senses can be used to investigate who has been visiting that territory and what food might lie within it.

In the absence of lots of exercise, food and feeding sometimes become prime objectives in life. Rather than living for exercise, some dogs live for food, and finding it becomes their main reason for being. When this happens, scavenging becomes even more than just self-rewarding, it becomes the reason for living.

32. Why do I have this compulsion to bury bones?

Burying bones is a sign of the dog's prehistoric past, when she saved food for days of famine. All dogs have the potential to bury bones but few do so.

Many canines only ever see bones on people's dinner plates. They are never given them because of the possible, though often exaggerated, dangers they present. Swallowed bone can produce constipation or even a complete intestinal blockage that can be relieved only through surgery. Boneless dogs still have the same bone-burying urges as other dogs, so they usually bury dog treats, chews and biscuits instead. When a garden isn't available, these deprived dogs try to bury objects in carpets, especially in corners, and frustratingly try to cover the 'buried' object by pushing the carpet with their nose.

Dogs with gardens will bury objects symbolically rather than practically, for they often forget about their buried objects and never dig them up. Some dogs will bury cats or squirrels they have killed, to let them ripen. Wild canines such as foxes bury bird eggs and later dig them up and eat them. Burying food protects it from other scavengers and provides a larder for times of want. Because dogs have lived on human handouts for so long, burying bones has become a symbolic rather than a practical activity.

33. Sometimes I have the urge to graze on grass just like a cow. I thought I was a carnivore. Does this mean that I'm really a closet vegetarian?

Although dogs are carnivorous and enjoy meat, they are not, like cats, dependent upon meat for survival. Grazing is perfectly normal, even beneficial.

Grass adds fibre to the diet. This bulks up the intestinal contents and helps it to pass through to the far end. Just as with humans, fibre in a dog's diet might be medically beneficial too, reducing the risk of bowel cancer. Rather than graze randomly, many dogs look for very specific grasses or weeds to eat. These herbivorous dogs prefer succulent new dew-covered spring grass to drier older forms. It is like a fresh green salad and the morning dew a bland vinaigrette. Later in the year it is not uncommon for dogs to graze on summer and early berries, especially blackberries. This isn't random behaviour but rather a selective choice on the part of the grazer.

Because they can manufacture essential fatty acids and amino acids themselves, unlike cats, dogs can survive on strictly vegetarian diets, although this is not how they have been designed to live. Vegetable-derived fats and proteins can form the building blocks that are necessary for life, but it is more difficult to ensure a proper balance of nutrients solely from plant rather than from both plants and animal sources. Dogs are really omnivores. They willingly try almost anything and many enjoy a light vegetarian meal on occasion.

34. Sometimes I gulp down my food so fast that I forget I've eaten. Is this dangerous?

Humans think it uncouth behaviour to gobble, but in the context of pack mentality it is a perfectly normal, acceptable and beneficial way to eat; for that matter, so is immediately regurgitating a meal and then eating it again.

Part of the behavioural baggage that dogs brought with them when they moved from the forest to the fireplace was competitive feeding. 'What you have I want' is one side of this, while vacuuming food without chewing or seemingly tasting it is another. Throwing large chunks into his mouth, a dog empties his food bowl within seconds, then looks up sadly at people to ask what magic made it disappear. People think this is absurd behaviour for a dog that has never had to compete with other dogs for his food. They forget that as far as the dog is concerned people are simply other large hairless dogs. He feels the need to compete with them even if they never get down on the floor and challenge for the food bowl.

Eating quickly is sometimes followed by regurgitation but this, too, is normal dog behaviour, especially among females who naturally regurgitate to feed their growing pups. Some dogs eat grass, not as a salad but to help regurgitate food. They do this when they feel stomach discomfort or simply to unload an overworked system.

35. Why do people get up and leave the room when I yawn?

Bad breath. Dogs don't mind having bad breath but people find it quite offensive. Although it can be created by the food that is eaten, in most instances bad breath means either mouth or digestion problems, most of which can be overcome.

Dogs smell of the food they eat. If they eat manure or fish, they smell of it. But if there are digestion problems smells can come from the stomach too. These dogs usually burp; if the burped smell is unpleasant it means that bacterial

fermentation or other smell-making activities are occurring in the stomach. If this is happening, the diet should be changed.

The most common cause of bad breath is gum inflammation resulting from calculus build-up on teeth. A dog's teeth yellow with age but chewing on skin and bones or brushing his teeth prevents mineral deposits from sticking to them. If a dog doesn't routinely massage his teeth and gums, a scummy slime forms on the gnashers and this thickens and becomes hard. Food catches between the build-up and the gums, bacteria multiply, and the dog's breath turns into a lethal weapon.

Bad breath usually means gum infection, which, in turn, means that each time the halitosis sufferer chews food he pumps bacteria into his bloodstream. While he is healthy and fit his defence system eliminates these germs, but when he is not, these circulating bacteria can produce a generalized infection and are thought to be involved in the most common form of heart disease.

Chapter Five
Travel

36. Why do I dribble whenever I get in a car?

Dribble is a sign of nausea. If dogs dribble in cars it means they want to be sick.

Motion sickness is common in young pups simply because car movement is an experience for which their sense of balance was not created. All four feet are meant to be permanently under a dog's control and firmly planted on the ground. Just as with humans, if pups are exposed to frequent and short car journeys, their balance mechanism evolves to cope with this type of motion.

Without early learning, motion sickness is more difficult to control. Adult dogs need several weeks' training to learn not to dribble or be sick when a car moves. They should get in a car, be rewarded for not dribbling and then get out. This should be repeated while the engine is running. Rewards follow for no dribbling with a little car movement and eventually with simple car trips. Training can be tedious and sometimes motion sickness tablets are a simple answer.

There are other circumstances in which dogs, tap-like, turn on their saliva glands. Some do it when they hear humans using can openers; others when they see peanuts, vitamin tablets or favourite foods. In these situations dogs expect to be fed so they start producing saliva. This can also be a reason why car riders dribble. Some adult dogs dribble in cars simply because they did so as pups. They no longer suffer from motion sickness but continue to dribble because it has become an ingrained habit.

37. People wear seatbelts when they get in the car. Shouldn't I wear one too?

Dogs are just as likely to be injured in car accidents as people are. Their problem is that most don't know how to release their seatbelts if they have to get out of the car quickly.

A dog should never travel on the front passenger seat of a car unless there are extraordinary reasons for doing so. Without the steering wheel for protection, this is the death seat. In an accident the dog is likely to be thrown forward and suffer substantial injuries.

She is far safer on a back seat. If the car suddenly stops, the dog is thrown against the back of the front seats. Injuries such as fractures are still common, however, because the dog falls into the foot well. Dog seatbelts are harness-like and prevent this type of dangerous forward movement. They attach to standard seatbelt latches and reduce injuries caused when the dog continues to move after the car has stopped.

Nosy and curious back-seat drivers, especially small terriers, enjoy climbing under the rear window for the best view. These small dogs become flying missiles when cars stop abruptly. Other canines have convinced people to buy station wagons especially for them. They like being able to get up and go for a little walk while travelling in the car. Firmly secured dog guards between the dog and passenger sections of the vehicle reduce the risk of injury to both parties.

38. I overheard people saying I'm going to be sent to kennels for a week. Friends have told me they are like prisons. What should I expect?

Kennel life is heaven for some dogs and hell for others. Dog-orientated dogs actively enjoy being sentenced to a week or more in kennels. They enjoy seeing, hearing and scenting other dogs. They become more alert, especially if they are

permitted to exercise with fellow inmates or even to room with them. Human-orientated dogs, on the other hand, can find forced living with other dogs extremely distasteful. For them, staying in kennels is a bit like an unathletic urban human being forced to go on a survival course.

Good kennels cater for both types of canine personality. Kennel units themselves should have warm indoor facilities as well as connected outdoor runs. They should be designed so that reclusive dogs can retire to secluded areas where they can't be seen, while extrovert dogs move to other parts of the kennels where they can see and communicate with other extroverts. This is easily achieved by having a platform in each kennel. Introverts have their beds under the platform, while extroverts spend most of their time on top of it.

Good kennel menus contain a choice of foods, including home-made, individually packaged TV dinners for truly picky eaters. Perhaps most important of all are the staff at the kennels. These people should be thoroughly inspected. The more questions *they* ask about a dog, the more likely they are to be considerate of an individual dog's specific needs and requirements.

39. I'm an inquisitive dog and would like to explore the world outside my garden. Is there any guaranteed way of my finding my own way home if I stray?

Most dogs that stray get lost and never find their way home. Canines navigate by using all of their senses. They remember sights, sounds and noises. If they don't come across any familiar ones, they get as lost as people do. Some panic and race back and forth not knowing what to do; others simply apply common sense and embark on a methodical search for anything familiar.

The most methodical dogs will work in ever increasing circles, sniffing ground and air scents for anything they recognize. When a familiar odour is found, they follow it until they realize where they are.

In almost every country there are stories of dogs finding their way home from hundreds of miles away. These dogs traverse rivers, mountains, deserts, cities, industrial landscapes and motorways to turn up finally, footsore but happy, on their own doorstep. Occasionally dogs manage to do this and it could be that they have an electromagnetic navigational ability like birds, but it is a one in a million chance. People relish these stories. They want to think that dogs can find their way home because they have enshrined the idea of canine loyalty in human folklore. The sad reality is that dogs get lost more easily than people do and in the absence of identification and human help are unlikely ever to find their way home.

40. What if I lose my dog tag? Are there any sure ways by which I can identify myself?

Dog tags bearing the dog's name and telephone number on permanently worn dog collars are the best means of identification. It is a good idea to have the veterinarian's telephone number on the tag, so that if a lost dog is found and her people are not home, the finders know who to contact for advice or medical attention. All veterinarians provide twenty-four-hour emergency cover so someone is always available.

Collars and tags go missing so it is a good idea for the dog to carry additional ID on her body.

The most common means are tattoos or microchip implants injected under the skin.

Tattooing an identification number in the ear is an easy, painless and cheap method of permanent identification. It works best when it is either part of a national dog registration scheme or is administered by a national organization such as a kennel club. When a tattoo-numbered dog turns up at a police station or dog shelter, a call to the registration centre identifies the dog and his most recent home address and telephone number.

The high-tech equivalent to tattooing is implanting a tiny microchip under the dog's neck skin. This is done by a simple injection. When a scanner is fanned over the dog, it 'reads' the microchip's information. This form of ID is only useful when all dog shelters and police stations scan dogs for implants. The unexpected bonus is that it is a tamper-proof form of identity in case of disputes.

41. Let's say I get lost, have no identification and end up in a dog shelter. What are my chances of coming out of there alive?

Miserable. Throughout Europe, North America and Australasia, dog shelters are forced to kill millions of dogs every year. Some are killed because they are elderly and unwell, others because they are dangerous, but the vast majority are healthy dogs destroyed simply because they have no ID and no people can be found who want to live with them.

Some charities have a 'no kill' policy. If a dog ends up in one of these shelters, he is kept as long as it takes to find a home for him. If he carries no ID but is young, active and intelligent, he might even join a training programme at another charity to become a 'hearing dog' and spend a stimulating life acting as ears for a profoundly deaf person. Otherwise he lingers in kennels built especially for long-stay inmates, always on show for people who might, one day, want to take him into their own home.

This is the exception rather than the rule. Unidentified dogs usually live for only days, or at the most weeks, after they enter a dog shelter. The luckiest are usually young pure-breds. For some curious reason these are the dogs most likely to be taken into a new home by the generous people who visit dog shelters. It's curious, because pure-breds are certainly no healthier than cross-bred or mongrel dogs. Because selective breeding increases the risk of inherited diseases, pure-breds often suffer from a wider range of possible problems than their less highly bred cousins. Pure-breds are not more intelligent either, although the personality traits of a pure-bred are easier to anticipate because these too can be inherited.

Upon arrival at the shelter dogs get a medical examination and treatment for any existing problems and then go on show. People come and look at them. The wisest dogs put on extra mascara, wag their tails as fast as they can and smile broadly as people pass by, but it is only the luck of the draw that decides which ones find new homes. Because there is such an overwhelmingly large and unending number of unidentified stray dogs, if shelter inmates can't convince people to take them home, they are soon killed to make way for the constant procession of others.

Chapter Six Grooming and Preventive Care

CHAPTER SIX

Grooming and Preventive Care

42. I like water on my own terms, not when people throw it on me. How often should I bathe and groom?

Many dogs take to water naturally. When they see muddy puddles they belly-flop in. These dogs enter every river, stream, pond or lake they come across for the simple exhilaration of practising their dog paddle. Swimming is enjoyed but bathing is endured. The difference is that the latter is forced upon a dog by people. As far as she is concerned, bathing is carried out not to make her clean but as a simple act of human dominance. No matter how much she likes the water, she hates it when she is not in control.

Dogs should swim as often as they like but bathe in soapy water infrequently because soap and detergent break down the natural oils in the fur. Bathing should be carried out when dogs stink or their fur is sufficiently dirty to require it. The need for soapy baths diminishes as the frequency of grooming increases. Dogs who are routinely brushed and combed rarely need to be bathed because regular grooming keeps the skin and fur in pristine condition. Some dogs, like birds, give themselves dust baths by rolling in sand or dry earth. This, too, is a marvellously effective and natural way to keep hair in the best condition. Long, thin-coated breeds need frequent grooming to prevent matts of hair forming, especially behind their ears and between their legs. Although licking is beneficial, they need active human help to groom effectively.

43. Should I use any special shampoo to eliminate body odour?

Dogs should use shampoos and conditioners that are most appropriate for the texture, density and length of their coats. For example, a wire-haired fox terrier should avoid conditioners if he wants to live up to his name, while a silky terrier should always use one after each and every shampoo.

If a dog is healthy and fit, he should not suffer from body odour. Routine brushing and combing prevents most smell. If he does smell strongly, there is usually a specific reason, for example an ear infection or, if he is a spaniel, a lip fold infection, and these should be treated appropriately.

General body odour can be related to diet, but dog smell is also exaggerated when the oil-producing glands that keep his hair shiny and waterproof go into over-production. When this happens his coat becomes oily or dandruffy and he should use an anti-dandruff shampoo. Selenium, coal tar and benzoyl peroxide shampoos are all used, but zinc pyrithion, which people often apply for dandruff, might be dangerous if used frequently. As an alternative to conditioners, dogs can use products called humectants on their coats. These increase the suppleness of their skin and reduce dandruff without making their hair oily. They can be used as frequently as is necessary.

44. Be honest, is there really anything terribly wrong with me biting my own nails?

There is nothing wrong with nail biting as long as a dog doesn't bite off so much that he makes his nails bleed; in fact, people are far more likely to do that. Medium- and large-sized dogs wear down their nails naturally and have no need to bite them until they are older and their nails grow longer. On the other hand, very small canines weigh so little that without frequent nail grooming theirs grow excessively long and interfere with walking and running.

A typical nail biter simply lies down and munches at his claws, biting off the sharp tips. Some munchers lie on their backs, using one paw to hold down the other for grooming. Most dogs, however, need human help with this procedure.

All pups should have their nails cut when they are between eight and twelve weeks old. Only the sharp point of the nail is cut off. This is best done with a nail clipper that uses a guillotine action. Clippers that crush, scissor-like, between

two blades can cause pain if nails are thick, as
they will be later in life.

Inside the nail there is living tissue and this is
what bleeds and hurts when it is accidentally
severed. It can be seen and avoided in pearly
lustred white nails, but is invisible within dark
nails. All weight-bearing nails get routine wear,
but dew claws have little activity or function, so
these need most attention, especially in breeds
such as the Pekinese where they frequently grow
back around themselves and can puncture the
skin. All nails should be inspected and groomed
monthly.

45. I've got worms and they make my bottom itchy. How did I get them and how can I get rid of them?

Tapeworm segments cause bottom itch because
they crawl in and out, producing irritation. A
dog's other worms – roundworms, hookworms
and whipworms – usually stay further inside
where they can cause considerable damage but no
itchiness.

To provide a home for a tapeworm a dog must
consume a tapeworm egg. This is most commonly
done by eating a flea that already contains the
egg. Uncooked fish can be a source of another
tapeworm; offal from sheep, goats, pigs, cattle,

or even kangaroo for that matter, is yet another source of tapeworm eggs. In the intestines, an egg matures into an adult worm which, if it is the common flea-transmitted tapeworm, then releases egg-filled segments which meander out of the dog's bottom. Once in the outside world these eggs are eaten by flea larvae; the larvae mature into adult fleas, which the dog accidentally eats while grooming himself, and the tapeworm life-cycle has been completed.

Roundworms, hookworms and whipworms either are picked up from the environment or are a gift to pups from their mother before they are born. They seldom cause anal irritation but are sometimes vomited or passed in the dog's stool. All of these worms can be virtually eliminated by routine worming and defleaing. Pregnant females should be wormed frequently before birth, pups wormed several times while still only a few weeks old and all dogs at least twice yearly.

46. How can I best control my terror and panic when I visit the veterinary clinic?

First impressions can last for ever and it is unfortunate that the first time a dog visits a veterinary clinic he gets stabbed in the back. This is an unavoidable unpleasantry, so his visit should in all other ways be made as enjoyable as possible.

Very often he is already frightened because he has just had his first car ride, he is with people he doesn't know and he hears other animal noises that signal distress or danger. In the best of all possible circumstances, the veterinary clinic should provide a clean area where the pup can be put down, if only to find his feet again. He will probably want to empty his bladder, and if at the same time he comes across a treat to sniff and eat his first impression will be a positive one.

People often transmit their own fear of visiting the doctor or dentist or veterinarian to their dog. Even young pups are exquisitely sensitive to

people's behaviour. Dog owners often worry needlessly that the vet will tell them their new pup is a dud, is riddled with parasites, has four left feet or is a rat in disguise. They worry that the pup will be frightened or experience pain. The young pup picks up the owner's feelings of apprehension and he gets nervous. People should act as relaxed as possible when taking a dog to the veterinary clinic.

Once he is on the examining table, the dog should be approached at his own level. He should be allowed to walk over to his examiner and carry out an investigation.

When this has been completed, the examiner can investigate him. Injections are more painful to some dogs than others. Breeds such as Labradors seldom notice that anything has happened, while Cavalier King Charles spaniels shriek as if the end of the world has come. As most dogs can't concentrate on two things at once, now is a good time for another food treat to be offered. An injection is given while the pup investigates or eats the food he has just discovered. If this first trip is turned into an enjoyable occasion, it will make future visits easier. At home people can open a dog's mouth, look in his ears, part his hair, lift his tail and in other ways examine him as the vet does. This is ultimately of importance because easy dogs get more complete medical examinations and that makes diagnosis faster and better.

47. I've never met a dog that has had distemper. Is vaccination really worth the pain?

Yes, it is. Twenty years ago distemper was a relatively common disease. It is only because of effective vaccination programmes that it is now so uncommon in many parts of the world. Where routine vaccination is not carried out distemper is still a frequent cause of illness and death.

The value of routine vaccination against rabies where that virus exists is obvious. Inoculation protects both dogs and humans. But there are many other diseases both local or national against which dogs can be protected. Leptospirosis is spread through rat urine. It kills people and dogs each year but prevention is simple through vaccination. Parvovirus didn't exist in dogs until the late 1970s when it suddenly spread around the world, wiping out complete litters overnight. This is easily controlled through vaccination as well. So, too, are virus hepatitis and causes of less important but still troublesome kennel cough. Protection against all of these diseases is incorporated into a single vaccine. If there are specific diseases that occur in certain regions, risk of contracting them can also be reduced through vaccination. Lyme disease spread by ticks, Bordatella, a whooping-cough-like kennel cough and other infections that occur either seasonally or regionally can be prevented through routine vaccination. It all boils down to an argument over which is preferable, prevention or cure. Today sensible dogs and people opt for the former.

48. Sometimes my nose is wet; at other times it is dry. Does it matter?

It doesn't matter one tiny bit. The state of the nose depends upon what a dog is doing or has recently been doing, as well as the type of climate.

Sleeping dogs frequently have dry noses; upon awakening they usually stretch their bodies and then lick their noses. A wet nose is useful because scent molecules are trapped in the moisture and can be inhaled either into the nasal chambers themselves or up into the vomeronasal organ where the sex scent is analysed. When dogs are exercising, their noses are usually wet because exercise is the pet dog's equivalent of hunting; scenting ability should be at its best then.

Dogs can't sweat the way people do and in the warm weather wearing fur can be oppressive. Heavy panting eliminates excess heat and moisture and here, too, the nose can be moderately useful. Moisture evaporates off a wet nose, but the appendage may be hot or cold depending upon the surrounding temperature. The same applies indoors. The only circumstances in which the state of the nose is important is when dogs have fevers. A cold wet nose usually means there is no fever. A hot wet nose can be normal or can indicate that body temperature is above normal. It is only of significance when dogs show other signs of illness.

49. I hate taking medicine. What is the least distasteful way of doing so?

Receiving medicine by injection is the most reliable way and, curiously, often the least distasteful. Sometimes, as when treating sugar diabetes, it is the only way that medicine can be taken. Insulin injections are given with a very thin needle under the skin on the neck, one of the least sensitive parts of the body. Because it is part of the daily routine and is relatively innocuous most dogs don't mind.

Many people have a deep aversion to needles. They don't like receiving medicine from them and hate the thought of giving medicine with them. That's why most drugs are in liquid, capsule or tablet form. Human preferences do not necessarily apply to canines. Some dogs think that taking medicine by mouth is the most horrific torture devised by humans. They clamp their jaws shut, refusing to open the necessary orifice, or, if they do open up, they try to clamp down on the fingers giving the medicine.

Liquids can be more difficult to consume,

especially if they are ladled into a dog's mouth with a spoon. Plastic syringes are useful as administrators. The syringe is filled with the liquid which is then gently squirted into the dog's mouth with care that none gets down the windpipe.

Capsules and pills can be more difficult. Small dogs, in particular, seem to have unexplored hidden recesses deep in their mouth cavities in which they can hide pills for hours before spitting them out. Special plastic pill pushers can be used but these are potentially dangerous. It is preferable to hide the medicine. Cubes of meat work wonders, as does Cheddar cheese, although some antibiotics should not be given with dairy products. If a dog refuses to eat and must have his medicine, there is no alternative for a human but to hold his mouth open towards the sky and to drop the offensive object as far down as possible.

The mouth should be clamped shut and the neck rubbed. Dry pills can be greased with vegetable oil. Alternatively, a few drops of water can be squirted into the clamped-shut mouth. A nose lick means the medicine has gone down. Because dogs should always 'come' on command, people should never call them for such unpleasant indignities as pill-giving.

50. Is there life after death?

You need a theologian rather than a veterinarian to answer that question. There is a unique difference between many human deaths and dog deaths in that active euthanasia is rare in the former but common with the latter. Because so many dogs are living for so long, people increasingly are forced to make life and death decisions about when a dog should die.

Death itself is very peaceful. A dog is simply given an anaesthetic and falls asleep. While he is asleep, his heart stops. Then, depending upon where he has lived and what people want, he is usually either cremated or buried.

In countries with Judaeo-Christian traditions some people feel there is an afterlife for themselves but not for their dogs. In one survey one in five felt that dogs have an afterlife, while over twice as many felt that they themselves would have life after death. There are different attitudes

elsewhere. In Japan surveys show equal numbers of people feel that dogs and people have souls and afterlives. The dog's cardinal advantage over humans is that throughout his life he doesn't think about an afterlife. He approaches the end of his natural existence with dignity and dies without needing answers. Many humans who believe in an afterlife, however, hope that when they finally get there, dogs will be waiting.

91

List of Questions

CHAPTER FOUR   Diet

CHAPTER FIVE   Travel

CHAPTER SIX   **Grooming and Preventive Care**

Index

INDEX

THE ROALD DAHL QUIZ BOOK

Richard Maher and Sylvia Bond

Where are whangdoodles, hornswogglers and snozzwangers to be found? What happened to Grandma when she drank George's Marvellous Medicine? What does the word grubber mean?

Become a Roald Dahl expert with this essential quiz book.

THE PUFFIN BOOK OF SPELLING PUZZLES

William Edmonds

Test your spelling skills and amaze your friends *and* your teacher by puzzling your way through this comprehensive collection of intriguing and perplexing puzzles. All the puzzles have been carefully designed to develop your spelling technique the FUN way.

BEETHOVEN'S SECOND

Robert Tine

The Newton family are quite happy as dog people. But never in a million years did George Newton think they would be puppy people.

Enter Beethoven, followed by his friend, Missy, and their four St Bernard puppies. They are cuter than cute and messier than anything. None the less, just like Beethoven, George and his family quickly grow to love them all.

It's a big thing to look after so many dogs. It's an even bigger thing when there are nasty people around who want to put the puppies into breeding kennels, which means it's down to Beethoven and George to save the day!

CARNIVAL OF THE ANIMALS AND OTHER POEMS

Mick Gowar

A parade of weird and wonderful creatures jamboree their way through this unusual collection of poetry, inviting you to join in their mad carnival. Pause for more reflective moments; meet the melancholic pianist, applaud the conductor, and be prepared for some nasty surprises when you discover what *really* happened to the rats and children of Hamelin Town!

A DOG SO SMALL
Philippa Pearce

For months, Ben Blewitt had been thinking about dogs. Alsatians, Great Danes, mastiffs, bloodhounds, borzois ... He had picked and chosen the biggest and the best from the dog-books in the Public Library. So imagine his disappointment when, for his birthday, Ben received not a dog but a *picture* of a dog. Ben's imagination soon got to work, though, and that's when his strange adventures began.

FREE WILLY
Todd Strasser

Willy is a mighty killer whale. Jesse is an eleven-year-old runaway who never had a real home. Together they form a very special friendship.

The star attraction at an amusement park, Willy is restless and longs to be reunited with his family at sea. The park owner, however, has decided that the whale is worth more dead than alive. Can Jesse free Willy before it's too late?

YOUR MOTHER WAS A NEANDERTHAL
Jon Scieszka

What better way to avoid doing maths homework than to take a trip (with the help of Joe's magic book) back to the Stone Age. The Time Warp Trio plan to wow their ancestors with modern inventions, like juggling balls, water pistols and Walkmans. But dinosaurs, dangerous cavewomen, tigers, earthquakes and woolly mammoths are just a few of their problems.

THE PUFFIN BOOK OF HORSE AND PONY STORIES
Edited by K. M. Peyton

The best of pony stories, classic and modern, is here in this exciting addition to *The Puffin Book of* ... series. K. M. Peyton, the author of the *Flambards* series among many award-winning books, has been a life-long horse enthusiast, and her selection is a treat for every horse and pony lover.

Famous stories such as *Smoky* and *National Velvet* are included alongside often overlooked but no less brilliant stories like *Another Pony for Jean* by Joanna Cannan and *Jump for Joy* by Pat Smythe, making this an unforgettable read.

HANDS OFF OUR SCHOOL!
Joan Lingard

Katy McCree and her friends are in an uproar: their one-teacher school in the Highlands of Scotland might be closed down! Every family in the village becomes involved in the fight to save the school. And by the time the spring arrives, the community has come up with a daring plan: parents, pupils and teacher will go to Edinburgh to confront the Director of Education himself – and they even end up on television!

VIDEO ROSE
Jacqueline Wilson

Rose is a video freak. Her idea of heaven is sitting in front of the video, with a packet of marshmallows resting on her tummy. Her worst nightmare is the video breaking down – which is what happens one day. Rose's whole life is changed by a strange old man who comes to mend the video, and at the same time gives her the power to rewind and fast-forward her own life.